The Boy from the Chemist
is Here to See You

'The year's exciting debut was Paul Farley, whose *The Boy
from the Chemist is Here to See You* won the Forward Prize.
Witty, tender, precise and playful, Farley charts aspects of modernity
in the day-to-day, making the apparently ordinary vivid and unusual.
He manages an elegiac note for parts of his Liverpudlian past, and for
all the sassiness, he isn't smugly knowing or fashionably weary'
ROBERT POTTS, *Guardian* Books of the Year

'This is a brilliant book and amazingly imaginative.
It's about the world we live in now, but equally about the world
of Farley's father, the window cleaner from whom he gets his
surreal perspectives. Read this outstanding collection'
THE JUDGES OF THE 1998 WHITBREAD POETRY AWARD

'Paul Farley's first collection is as sharp as its title . . . Farley
attempts the most difficult climb of all, into the life of another, and
his glittering cleverness is always grounded in feeling'
HELEN DUNMORE, *Observer*

PAUL FARLEY

The Boy from the Chemist

is Here to See You

PICADOR

Acknowledgements are due to the editors of the following publications in which some of these poems first appeared: *Independent*, *The North*, *Observer*, *Poetry Review*, *The Printer's Devil*, *Scratch*, *Thumbscrew*, *Verse*.

'Laws of Gravity' won first prize in the 1995 Arvon International Poetry Competition and was published in the anthology of that name. 'Monopoly' appeared in a *TLS/Poems on the Underground* pamphlet in 1996.

The author wishes to thank the artist Kerry Stewart for the title of this book.

Contents

Eaux d'Artifice

The moon we know from dreams or celluloid
is high tonight. A dried-up fountain bed
gawps back, a baroque radio telescope
the race has left behind, always on the up,
defying gravity. The park seems of an age
that tried, in other small ways, to oblige
the same imperative – this domed palm-house
that brought the sky down closer; these dark yews
clipped conically and pointed heavenwards;
and fountains that suspended arcs and cords
of water, one so powerful it could hold
the weight of terrified cats or 'a Small Childe'
in its jets. The water only comes here now
to rest after the dream-days spent in cloud,
to swill round with the leaves and empty cans,
and then moves on. Its work is never done,
like man's, a thought that brings me back to earth:
soaked through with sweat, under her bone-light,
bouncing my signals back and forth all night,
the moon drowns out a point low in the south
that could be Mercury or the Eutalsat,
though these days she in turn has to compete
with our restless nightside. When I can't sleep
I walk these rhododendroned paths that keep
to strict ideas of sunset and sunrise,
and find my level on a bench, like this.

Depot

You wouldn't know a place like this existed.
It shows the street its modest, oily features
(a door I walked right past on my first day),
but opens into hangar-like proportions.
Here are the bays where dustcarts spend their evenings,
where grit summers, dreaming of Januaries,
and barriers mesh like deckchairs off-season.

I've dreamt of something like this sorting-house,
and walked its film-set streets, and tried its swings
some nights – the perfect playground, deserted –
but didn't know a place like this existed;
that crippled boys who stood outside our chemists
would form ranks like a terracotta army
in lives beyond thalidomide and weather.

Was this what lay behind the knowing winks
I caught between binmen, or am I dreaming
that road sweepers held doctorates in philosophy;
and knew, after the miles behind a big broom,
they would return to worlds not unlike this one,
find a spotless bench, and read their *Echo*
in the irony of strip lights over street lamps.

Termini

We lived where buses turned back on themselves,
when drivers still referred to us as 'scholars',
winding on their final destination
and we would end up here: PIER HEAD.
Today, a spinning blade blows *surf 'n' turf*
from a steakhouse kitchen, luring those
with appetites sharpened by river air
after a windswept round trip on the ferry.
What else is there? The city has shrunk back
from the front, slowly, over the years
leaving this airy strand the buses bypass,
and now nobody's journey into town
ends with a top-deck, front-seat panorama.
I left the slashed seat and the listing bottle
to finish this journey on foot, in the rain,
the same route where the brothers Lumière
cranked the first nitrate from a moving train;
and stand now where we sagged the long school day
eating hot dogs, watching buses turn
back to the far estates with lower case names,
an audience staying put for the minor credits.

Electricity

It comes as a shock to that first audience.
The street they walked in off just moments before
hangs pale on the wall. All the colour has gone,
and its faces and carriages have ground to a blur.

Remember, no one has thought of pianos
or credits. The performance will start off mid-scene,
once each hard bench is filled, when the first usher nods
and the lamp is turned up and the crank starts to turn

and their hairs stand on end to a shimmer of leaves
or the movement of clouds, and the way that the tense
has been thrown like a switch, where the land turns
    to dreams,
and where, sad to say, we have been living since.

A Thousand Hours

There were false starts, but life, for me, really
began the night he unplugged the telly
and snuffed the pilot light. As last-man-out
he worked right through to dawn, between the street
and this bedroom, until he'd stripped it bare,
but left me in his rush to check the meter,
to turn the stopcock on a copper tank,
count stairs and memorize that manhole's clunk,
the first hawked phlegm, the way a window pane
was answering the early Lime Street train;
and posted back his keys to nobody.

I've hung here naked since, by day barely
able to force a shadow to be thrown.
It's nights I come into my own:
a halo for the ceiling, corners for mice,
and through the glass a phantom of all this,
a twin star that is shedding kilowatts
in translation. Beyond these dark outskirts
my creator sleeps. I recall how his eyes
would whirr just like this night-time visitor
that might outlive me. Of all his ideas
I burn on, having been conceived in error.

Laws of Gravity

(for Julian Turner)

I found a guidebook to the port he knew
intimately – its guano-coated ledges,
its weathervanes, his bird's-eye river view
of liner funnels, coal sloops and dredgers.
It helped me gain a foothold – how he felt
a hundred rungs above a fifties street,
and whether, being so high, he ever dwelt
on suicide, or flummoxed his feet
to last night's dance steps, still fresh in his head.
It's all here in his ledger's marginalia:
how he fell up the dark stairwell to bed
and projected right through to Australia;
and said a prayer for rainfall every night
so he could skip his first hungovered round.
The dates he's noted *chamois frozen tight
into bucket*. When he left the ground
a sense of purpose overtook and let
a different set of laws come into play:
like muezzins who ascend a minaret
to call the faithful of a town to pray.
Take one step at a time. Never look down.
He'd seen the hardest cases freeze halfway,
the arse-flap of their overalls turn brown.

As a rule, he writes, *your sense of angle*
becomes acute at height. A diagram
he's thumbnailed shows a drop through a triangle
if you miscalculated by a gram.
Sometimes, his senses still blunted from booze,
he'd drop his squeegee, watch it fall to earth
and cling onto the grim hypotenuse
of his own making for all he was worth.
He seems to have enjoyed working that hour
the low sun caught the glass and raised the ante
on every aerial, flue and cooling tower,
and gilded the lofts, the rooftop shanty
town, when everything was full of itself,
and for a while even the Latin plaques
ignited with the glow of squandered wealth.
At times like these I see what our world lacks,
the light of heaven on what we've produced
and here some words lost where his biro bled
then *clouds of dark birds zero in to roost.*
There's IOUs and debtors marked in red
and some description of the things he saw
beyond the pane – a hard-lit typing pool,
a room of faces on some vanished floor
closed off and absolute like a fixed rule.
His story of the boy butting a wall,
the secretary crying at her desk,
all happened in the air above a mall.
Each edifice, each gargoyle and grotesque,

7

is gone. The earliest thing I remember:
as our van dropped a gear up Brownlow Hill
I looked back at the panes of distemper
that sealed a world. We reached our overspill,
and this is where our stories overlap.
The coming of the cradle and sheet glass
was squeezing out the ladder and the slap
of leather into suds, and less and less
work came through the door. And anyway
you were getting too old for scaling heights.
Now, when I change a bulb or queue to pay
at fairs, or when I'm checking in for flights,
I feel our difference bit down to the quick.
There are no guidebooks to that town you knew
and this attempt to build it, brick by brick,
descends the page. I'll hold the foot for you.

Era

Hide some under the carpet, line a drawer
so they will know about us, who we were
and what we did on one day years ago,
our births and deaths, our sales and tide tables.
Make a mental note of sizes no one
has seen or heard of, before it's too late –
Colombier, Imperial, Elephant –
and though the forests exhale a long sigh
of relief, what hope is there for this page
you're reading now? Cash in your mattressed wads:
they cease to be tender as of midnight.

The Alphabet

We arrived at night with nothing to declare,
a school of thought, though to your officials
we travelled light – a snap-case stuffed with clothes,
toothbrush, some useless coins, pencils and pens.
I wondered how I'd ever been homesick
for somewhere I'd never lived – pigeons, rainlight,
the nacreous squares darkened with plane trees –
then set about erasing what I'd read.
Your full beam picks the roadsign's sans serif
out of the dark hedgerows; your newspaper
has changed its fonts; the words have space to breathe,
your people fresh air, high in concrete blocks.
We made our mark. You'll be surprised to hear
these days our talents lie elsewhere – a ditch,
the drawing board of claim forms – having bid
a fond farewell to orphans, widows, bastards,
to p's and q's, hot metal. Now my friends
the architect and the 'father of modern typography'
beg in the soft drizzle beneath the displays
that scroll and refresh ideas of heaven, a plea
for food and shelter handwritten on cardboard
in words that no longer 'leap out' at anybody.

A Carry-On

Industry had a sex life once. From this train
it hides its other history well – nooks and haunts
overlooked by the quick tour or annual report.
Behind the windows that spell out T-O-L-E-T,
up stairwells, past perimeter fencing,
they are still at it. Beneath dorsal rooftops

they have clocked on and are shagging.
They are shagging inside the rendering plant,
the derelict zipper factory, inside storage sheds
lit all night by kliegs. They are orgying, in fact,
unhindered by crabs, or doses of the clap,
fucking the arse off each other in acres of complex.

Somewhere inside that major distribution centre
overalls lie strewn on the boardroom floor,
blinds drawn, and a secretary leans forever
into a low tier. Pirelli calendars have nothing
on a room in Fort Dunlop where a secret knock
admits one, to shag, all night if they want.

A whole workforce, shagging – each echelon
from the management down. You think you glimpse
tantric shapes in the sodium dark as you pass,
but the workforce are long since laid off, sent home
and have gone to their beds, all alone. The train you are on
won't wake those who never-had-it-so-good.

Aquarius

More fool you who believe in the end of decades.
The seventies live on in top-floor flats
you can't see in for overgrown pot plants;
where someone struggles to crack a dial-band set
and Che stares down onto an unmade bed.

Letters pile up, shoring the front door
like a drift. Mung shoots replenish themselves
and the tap water's good for ages yet.
They never leave the room or check the view.
The neighbours wonder, as they come and go,

at such bad taste in music and curtains;
but eventually come to admire such cool retro.
Behind closed doors there is low talk of scurvy
as they carve a dice from the dwindling oatcake
cast years ago inside a chest of drawers.

After they tune out their hair will grow, for a while,
and the plants will still pull to the sun, until
the soil cracks and dries. Then, and only then,
will the old decade die, and your amazing nineties
shed its light; its seen-it-all-before light.

from 'Songs for Swingeing Lovers'

Living in Sin

Hide the pink toothbrush, the dark nest of knickers,
the loofah, the fake fur, the eau de toilette;
sling all that yoghurt and climb in this cupboard:
they're trying to cut off our benefit.

Bacon and Eggs

Breakfast. In a fat-splashed gown
        your working model fitted:
'The chicken is only involved
        but the pig, the pig is committed.'

Treacle

Funny to think you can still buy it now,
a throwback, like shoe polish or the sardine key.
When you lever the lid it opens with a sigh
and you're face-to-face with history.
By that I mean the unstable pitch black
you're careful not to spill, like mercury

that doesn't give any reflection back,
that gets between the cracks of everything
and holds together the sandstone and bricks
of our museums and art galleries;
and though those selfsame buildings stand
hosed clean now of all their gunk and soot,

feel the weight of this tin in your hand,
read its endorsment from one Abram Lyle
'Out of the strong came forth sweetness'
below the weird logo of bees in swarm
like a halo over the lion carcass.
Breathe its scent, something lost from our streets

like horseshit or coalsmoke; its base note
a building block as biblical as honey,
the last dregs of an empire's dark sump;
see how a spoonful won't let go of its past,
what the tin calls back to the mean of its lip
as you pour its contents over yourself

and smear it into every orifice.
You're history now, a captive explorer
staked out for the insects; you're tarred
and feel its caul harden. The restorer
will tap your details back out of the dark:
close-in work with a toffee hammer.

Dependants

How good we are for each other, walking through
a land of silence and darkness. You
open doors for me, I answer the phone for you.

I play jungle loud. You read with the light on.
Beautiful. The curve of your cheekbone,
explosive vowels, exact use of cologne.

What are you thinking? I ask in a language of touch
unique to us. You tap my palm *nothing much*.
At stations we compete senses, see which

comes first – light in the tunnel, whiplash down the rail.
I kick your shins when we go out for meals.
You dab my lips. I finger yours like Braille.

My Italics

On waking disappointed from deep sleep,
he'll boot up his machine, sit down and type:

Even though I know that I will never
live the rural life, God knows I've tried
to imagine rising at five in bad weather
carrying a paraffin lamp, peering inside
a fecund dark, up to my elbows in lather
helping pull a shiny calf from its mother.
But five o'clock comes round just once most days.
Deep in quilt, I'm stuck for raw material.
The lamp slips from my hands. After each blaze
I'll stumble from its ashes to my cereal . . .

His inkjet ploughs the page for all it's worth:
it drops head-first, the easiest of births.

The Colonists

From the same deck we stood on observing
the test at Bikini, wearing dark shades,
I can hear music below – some of the crew
drunk on white rum from the stores,
jiving to a mono Dansette
while its needle tries to stay on course.

I had orders to land at Liverpool
and find dockside shebeens so the boys
could trade our shiny, ocean-worn 45s;
but each joint had its smartass –
wisecracking, putting sales at risk
by picking out some surface noise, or worse,
holding them oblique in paraffin light
to check for scratches – I had to put them right:

each click was formed within a tilting swell,
each drizzle patch describes a squall of spray;
every disc is playing something else
beyond its backbeat and its middle eight.

It went round like this long into the night;
offering tobacco, I told them how
a sound would fan out from this port one day,
how there'd be sea-lanes of bluejeans bound
for Minsk and Kiev, how records would burn

like bibles. But they only laughed.
One even asked if I'd take a *polygraph*.

I smiled – his use of that word in itself
meaning our B-movies were having some effect.

Crazy Golf

They still come on mornings like this to the waste ground,
same ratty overcoats, same choice of one club,
accepting the Mulligans sportingly granted
by nobody, slicing off into the rough
with two sulky lurchers in tow. All around
lie the mind's out-of-bounds – a ditch, a road,
a fence to the swing-park – here it's the Open
or Masters. They know

                         the range of their short iron
or taped-up wood, birdy the burnt-out car
some days, nod when they get round under par:
and know, in time, all fairways turn to this;
that we'll play here again, come rain or shine,
kiss goodbye to our dimpled gutta-percha
and squint to see the links where there are none,
every single stroke a hole in one.

Papal Visit

If Manchester is fogbound it would mean
his plane getting diverted into Speke.
No doubt he'll kiss the tarmac, cross himself
then join the motorcade. What time is it?
He might take this route if the traffic's bad
on Menlove Avenue and drive past here,
past the spotlit five-a-side cage, past
the row of scorched shop units, past the pub
with two dogs on the roof, and if he does
he'll surely wonder at the poor turnout
who'll wave from stops and bannerless buildings
half-heartedly; he'll surely marvel
at the kid who'll wander up for two cornets
at the lights. Am I the only one
seeing to it? – rushing from flat to flat
along the way, handing out candles,
establishing sight lines and vantage points,
checking the sheet-steel door of the chippy
is high enough to admit staff and censer,
it being Friday, and a long flight from da Vinci.

Why Waitresses Cry

All afternoon the chicane ribboned offside
lit by our headlights. And I pulled over
after nearly taking us up the verge at eighty.
Coffee. More coffee. Chain smoking.
The games arcade roared with the fury of drivers
flouting the laws of Euclidean space.
I almost killed us all dreaming of you,
up the M4 with your three-hour lead.

My passengers said I should get my head down.
I did. *And I was a short order waitress*
sidling from kitchen to table with notepad
in hand, trying to write, in between the demands
of an egg-cracking cook and his customers,
in that shorthand a doctor, dead on his feet,
might employ; or a love-note, slid on a coaster
across the slops and ash of an evening.

And I carried the laminate, ersatz hidebound
menu to your table, and asked what you wanted,
or whatlyubehavin? And you recognized me,
even dragged up in gingham and paper hat,
saw me coming. But neither of us broached it
and so we went through the ritual of ordering;
your sunny-side-up to my scribbling and nodding.
Clearing, I found a butt stubbed in a yolk.

The car starts from cold. We press on in silence.
England's most wipered, American state
in between services, runs off the windscreen.
Further ahead now, your junction, your turn-off,
and I'll keep my foot down until we reach London.
But not before several dangerous re-screenings
are attempted. I catch myself, in the rear-view:
My name's Paul. I'll be your waitress this evening . . .

Sister

It's gone quiet – there is no more cursing
at the TV as his horse hits the fence.
The weather doesn't *turn gangster*, simply worsens,
a black cloud moving in front of the sun.

We go to bed when we please – don't run for his fags,
his bets, don't eat in silence. Set the canary free –
we don't need it risking his outhouse stink,
bouyant filter tip, offensive whistling . . .

And please, don't reject me when I come clean
and admit I've stolen his wink,
his facial tic. Don't be too quick to judge
my voice as it drops to his octave,

employs the odd *kibosh, cahoots, buckshee*.
Catch his myoclonic jerk
from a seconds-old dream about lifts or kerbs.
Something of him informs something of me.

Extract

'In Kandy, ancient capital of Ceylon,
there is a temple dedicated to
a single tooth. Backpackers chance upon
the pink-lit shrine, to leave sandal and shoe
at the entrance, find the small canine,
and wonder how all this grew around it.
And some, still feverish despite quinine,
might sip the rosewater and then anoint
themselves . . .'

                I paraphrase a magazine
found in a waiting room with time to kill
and reconstruct that pebble-dashed end-house
where, twice a year, I waited in the smell
of antiseptic, burning bone and gas.
I learned my lines in earshot of the drill

and came round to my name, the nurse's slap.
Despite chanting the travel article,
my tongue explored a new, salty gap;
and I took the tooth to bed with me that night
but did not wake in scented candlelight.

Monopoly

We sat like slum landlords around the board
buying each other out with fake banknotes,
until we lost more than we could afford,
or ever hope to pay back. Now our seats
are empty – one by one we left the game
to play for real, at first completely lost
in this other world, its building sites, its rain;
but slowly learned the rules or made our own,
stayed out of jail and kept our noses clean.
And now there's only me – sole freeholder
of every empty office space in town,
and from the quayside I can count the cost
each low tide brings – the skeletons and rust
of boats, cars, hats, boots, iron, a terrier.

Real Life Television

Viewer, I resisted: not for the windowbox of skunk
or nugget in tinfoil for personal use;
not the drawers turned out on the lino
or sniffer dog spooking my mongrel. No,
what got me was the dream they crashed in on.

The one about running away. As always
a moon shone over the block's sculpted hush,
each landing was salted to ward off frost
and milk bottles were left out in pairs
like hotel shoes. I got further than ever

this time, in colour, but a door I never saw
opened. Lights, cameras, action,
a torch in my eyes and my name, bleeped.
Some residents stood at their doors and smiled
as they led me away, the caretaker bribed.

I can never go back. I resisted,
I admit it. There I am, bound and trussed,
verité, screaming abuse. Viewer, squint at my face –
blurring, bitmapped – a hive of ideas
trying to focus on that other thing, that place.

Darkroom

In the vinegary air, in the safety light,
a high-rise fixes in a tray
and is pegged to drip-dry on a line
with the others taken yesterday:

the lift-shafts and the rubbish chutes
the *Echo* sent you to record.
Right now – you check your luminous
wristwatch – evacuees applaud

a cloud of dust clearing to show
an unexpected view, the blast
punched out to the faintest of echoes;
the birds coming back, confused and lost.

But something is wrong. In the developer
a room is forming you never entered.
Such detail – *Spiderman* wallpaper,
biro scrawl – you would have remembered.

Focused to the molecule
you're locked behind its squat-proof door.
Your itinerary has gone to the wall
and here, on the thirteenth floor,

no one can hear. The last street light
barely penetrates. They left a clock.
The room takes shape. You watch and wait,
the charges primed in the damp breezeblock.

A Minute's Silence

The singing stops. Each player finds his spot
around the ten-yard circle that until
tonight seemed redundant, there just for show.
The PA asks us to observe the hush.

We find we're standing in a groundsman's shoes,
the quiet he must be familiar with
while squeaking chalk-paste up the grassy touch,
or overseeing a private ritual

and scattering the last mortal remains
of a diehard fan beneath each home-end stanchion.
No one keeps a count or checks their watch
so space is opened up. It seems to last

a small eternity – the happy hour
that stretches to three, the toast, the final spin.
I observe the silence sneak through turnstiles
and catch on quick – a bar muffles its pumps;

in function rooms, a wedding reception
freezes still as its own photograph;
an awful bagwash winds down mid-cycle –
a Saturday gridlocked, unaccompanied

by hooters or sirens. Like early audiences
we have left the street to its own devices

to watch the flicking shadow of itself
onscreen, the purring spool somehow apart

from all of this. It leaves the one-way system
and finds less work to do outside of town:
a rookery, light aircraft, and the wind
banging gates or moaning through the lines.

(How still without birdsong. It still guts me
to think of all the havoc wreaked each spring
we combed the hedges outside our estate
and stole the still-warm clutches from each nest;

all that music, blown and set in file
on sawdust in a two-pound biscuit tin,
displayed to rivals in attack formation,
a 4–3–3 of fowls and passerines.)

Sooner or later silence reaches the coast
and stops just short of getting its feet wet.
There's something of the Ice Age to all this.
The only sound's the white noise of the sea

that is all song, all talk, all colour, mixed.
Before that whistle bursts a hole and brings
the air rushing back in with arc lighting,
calls for owners of the double parked,

the last verse of 'You'll Never Walk Alone'
(never . . . *the sweet silver song of a lark*)

listen, to where the shore meets the salt water;
a million tiny licking, chopping sounds:

the dead, the never-born, the locked-out souls
are scratching on the thin shell we have grown
around ourselves. Listen. The afternoon
is dark already, and there is a moon.

Without Potatoes

'Without potatoes we would be like loose threads on a loom,
for potatoes are what bind life together.' – Amarayan proverb

We took spud guns onto the terraces,
Threw King Edwards spiked with razor blades.
Ate chips salted and vinegared,
Burnt our cheeks on the polished nickel, waiting.

We danced the mashed pah-tay-tah;
Wrestled with earthy sackfuls
Dropped from chutes on childhood errands;
Watched the roasty fall from ubiquity
On Sundays centered round gas ovens
To french fries, Spud-U-Like and waffles.

I miss the simple pleasures – of rinsing
A tuber under a cold tap; of coiling the peelings
Into a bucket; of gouging the eyes out.
I never thought I'd come to say such things.

Permanent

What lasts, and for how long, and what's the point?
The years spent puckering a hog's-hair brush
between his lips had to exact a price.
The final months were full of wild invention:
the colours of the Fauves, painterly space
opened . . . all in that little studio
before the century turned, though no one went

and looked. No one, except his old patrons,
delivering a still life or a nude
from forty summers back, for putting right;
who ignored the old man's abstractions:
this turpentine was spirited from some wood,
I hear its glassy sap, the mineral chink
of pigment locked in ore beyond the light

before these worldly allusions – all surface,
they jabbed their fingers to a model's skin
or fruit on its slow fade back to compost.
The bright chromatics first. Even so, don't think
the days he left his palette in the sun
to chase those fugitives have gone to waste.
He lives among them now. There is no peace.

Retrospective

1. *Stubs.* 1989, aluminium, wood, glass, stainless steel, monitors, betting slips, cigarettes (smoked), silkscreen reproduction of the bay filly *Molly Longlegs*

2. *Sisyphus.* 1990, 30° inclined escalator (set to descend), tank, aerator, water, any anadromous fish of the Salmonidae family

3. *Odds.* 1992, refrigerated vitrium, fluorescent light, the artist's semen (note: at temperatures of $-2°$ to $-4°$C, this is malleable as putty)

4. *The Optic Nerve is a Lazy River.* 1993, telescope (8-inch reflector, altazimuth mounting), perspex, Mersey Yellow Pages (on microfiche)

5. *Waveform.* 1995 (lost), franking machine, sealed air Jiffy, brace of Manx kippers, first class postage within mainland UK

Velvets, Can, Stooges

For John, in the hope he is still alive
somewhere. An album is nearing its dead centre
in the room where we camped with a Primus stove,
lit by the glow of a one-bar heater.
At that moment the page becomes a strain
to read, and as quick as a summer
can end with the drawing of a curtain

he is there, in a past that squats at my shoulder,
teaching me the litany of bands
and a way to fold with three Rizla;
there, the same slender plugwired hands
that were gentle with charcoal
those afternoons in the Life Room,
but hard on himself with a shared needle.

In the hope that he has turned the flame
to one more item of luggage:
has burned the phone numbers and names
old as a habit, page by page:
that he sees a world beyond the door's
one-eyed, dilated view.
There are burnished spoons in the drawer

where I live now. I stole a thing or two
and entertain the idea
still, in light like this, then forget you

like some character in the book
that's slipped from my lap. You were so real then
that I almost looked for those records you took,
and put on that arctic winter again.

Epic Soundtracks

'Put the needle on the record . . .' – Trad

Our dream shop lies at the end of a disused line:
a seafront window full of light and gulls,
a door rigged to a bell, one of those signs
the owner flips between OPEN and CLOSED
as regularly as the tide. It lies beyond
the last frames of 'London to Lime Street in Four Minutes',
is unvisited off-season, and hides its trove
of mint plastic, foxed inner sleeves, white labels:
such riches. And the owner doesn't know it.
We'll rent the room upstairs and start to mine
its rarities, which see the light of day
after the unplayed years compressed in racks,
and before that, in a walnut radiogram
or car-boot sale. If they have weathered well,
in darkness, as the best do, then we'll pay.
These daylit nights we hold an acetate
up to the net curtains to judge its grade
(like Elvis at Sam's store on Union)
and bear it like a chemist boy's black box
up to our room, then have to listen, once . . .

the stylus makes dark swarf of the King's voice.
In every trawl I find something I've lost
(or still own – here's the biroed tinker's mark

you left inside each flap that day you sold
the lot). Now ask the guy to put it on.
A hiss and rumble has leaked in, like rain
into my shoes. The meter's peaks and troughs
could be a poem's, turned onto its side,
the overflow spattering the sill those nights
we lay awake. The traffic's steady roar
reminds me that you've gone. My first summers

were lullabied like this, and rock and roll
of course, in its own infancy, naive
as lamé, solid-state. Each day would last
its own lifetime . . . but I've been over this
so many times the thoughts have worn a hole.
It's times like this the mind's dark search-engine
goes screeching back across the grain of years
to one review I wrote, this time displayed
as newsprint turning jaundiced on a fridge.
Some lines are clear, despite the encryption:

'This hasn't happened since Kraldjursanstalen's
"Scarce Kant" . . . on each and every song . . .
it sounds like they recorded this in heaven
then sent the tapes to hell for mastering,
booked studio time by phases of the moon . . .
the bass-line's brutalist, amphibian squall . . .
dislocated . . . beats of blunted soul,
darkside dub, the urban freakscape tunes
of "Snowflakes Falling on the International Dateline"

with Spector or King Tubby as producer . . .
not music, more time-stretched hallucination . . .
Ladies and gentlemen, we have left Earth's atmosphere . . .'

O Coriolis, what hemisphere am I in?
I ask the sink, which glares back, swallowing
warm piss, and fumbling back to nylon sheets
descend again.
                Back in that other room
we cricked our necks trying to find a spine
along the rows of shelving neatly filled.
One night we reached a kind of equinox:
those records matched the hours we had left.
And then we passed a point of no return
without knowing which album tipped the scales,
what moment – just a cloud across the sun,
a tingle as you slot it into place . . .

Our histories could fill a megastore
on this side – soul, billowing through windows;
the tinny overture played down your ear
that day the bank refused an overdraft;
a cub music reporter for the *Echo*,
who can't believe the dictaphone's bullshit;
the voices that you can't put faces to
(here's Mrs Murphy, fishing a boiled sweet
from down your throat, calmly, as you turned blue);
and more, much more. Each dawn chorus we've heard,
hours of grunts and glossolalia,

and every thunderclap we've counted in
is slipped out of its antistatic sleeve
and played.

Some nights our music blew too loud:
we couldn't sleep. You couldn't stand the noise
and walked, taking your share, and some of mine.
Tonight, for all I know, my old records
play to a petrol sunset in New York
or dawn in Kyoto . . .

I've drifted off,
but this time pull away to that true centre,
to where the unique lies in its dumb corner
that the world has bypassed, the sea not returned to.
Here is one final disc, cut anticlockwise.
I'll smell it, sad as the dark of my first school desk,
and hold it up oblique to that bright window,
where it yields no other stories but its own –
no favourite track, worn down and crestfallen,
but a careful owner. I will not be satisfied
until we cross into that salted region,
the dark grooves' undertow taking us right out
beyond the shiny lip of the horizon.

'Cream'

If Melville and Hawthorne had taken the same drugs
what would they have made of the counting-houses
all suddenly full of lasers and bass drums
that pummel the sternum and stop down the iris?

What would they have made of this light show's finale
unexposed, as they were, even to the flashbulb,
or amplified breakbeats through 20K sound rigs
and scantily clad boys and girls going apeshit?

Unaccustomed, as they were, to front-of-house etiquette
how would they get past the private security
decked out in cummerbunds, high hats, fob watches
(hands swapped like compasses turned in a thunderstorm)?

How would they get past the offers for 'love doves'
or know how to dance in the amorphous mass
that's peaking as one to the sum total effect,
without any handbags to act as a focus?

Documentarist

It's clear I love the footage of the past:
its herring catches, silvery flinders
that flap in unimagined elements,
the miner's face that bares bright teeth and eyes
to camera, the skies scribbled and crossed
by a century's dust. A cold, unglamorous

photography no starlet or leading man
could feel at home for long in. Peeling walls,
five to a bed . . . See how they're smiling still
from deep inside their mould-invaded tins –
a porterage through equatorial damp,
incisors flared. Look back into this lens

beyond the here-and-now, to darkened rooms:
the future screens its ideas of us,
to rows that multiply back endlessly.
Smile, as they file out to a world
of worked-out seams, depopulated seas,
the ancient shock of daylight still playing.

The Lamp

(At sea, Dec 29. 1849)

Aboard, at home again, this book closes.
No written record of that westbound voyage
survives. I have you travelling with the sun
and mangy Irish packets, dreaming up
your story. Five weeks berthed alone, below
the waterline, immersed in printed matter
from Holborn, Charing Cross Road, and the Strand.
Was it like this? The artificial glow
of sperm oil lit those words across the miles
of ocean swells. Having the presence of mind,
you saw yourself, a reader in the dark,
dependant on the whale's 'sweet grass butter'.
The lamp hung true despite the pitch and roll.
You had the shortest chapter by landfall.

To a Minor Poet of 1965

(after Borges)

The hour that lies in wait at the day's close
that stops the world dead like a frozen stream,
when scales fall from our eyes and it would seem
the sun has caught our most attractive pose:

a man might pause to think he has lived out
a lifetime here, then blush with self-regard
and board his bus to find a window seat . . .
but hold that moment when he dropped his guard:

Between the crossword and the *Echo*'s edge,
between two stops. A shorter time than that.
A moment locked into these words' designs.

I fold back to our raincoat's secret stitch
your complete works and claim my window seat,
the streets ringing with paper vendors' lines.

Keith Chegwin as Fleance

The next rung up from extra and dogsbody
and all the cliches are true – days waiting for
enough light, learning card games, penny-ante,
while fog rolls off the sea, a camera
gets moisture in its gate, and Roman Polanski
curses the day he chose Snowdonia.

He picked you for your hair to play this role:
a look had reached Bootle from Altamont
that year. You wouldn't say you sold your soul
but learned your line inside a beating tent
by candlelight, the shingle dark as coal
behind each wave, and its slight restatement.

'A tale told by an idiot . . .' 'Not your turn,
but perhaps, with time and practice . . .', the Pole starts.
Who's to say, behind the accent and that grin,
what designs you had on playing a greater part?
The crew get ready while the stars go in.
You speak the words you'd written on your heart

just as the long-awaited sunrise fires
the sky a blueish pink. Who could have seen
this future in the late schedules, where I
can't sleep, and watch your flight from the big screen;
on the other side of drink and wondering why,
the zany, household-name years in between?

Not Fade Away

A cornfield deep in drifts. I walked an hour
without moving. The outskirts of a town
that felt, with all its ploughed streets and neon,
like stepping from a page. I found a bar
and tried to force a boilermaker down.
The barman asked if I was twenty-one.

You don't crawl free from crashes every day.
In celebration of that windchilled night
I've pissed the intervening years away
in dark corners, doorways, and come so far
from all those screaming girls, the cold limelight
winks back faint as a star.

No one believes the bore who doesn't wash
or listens to the stories he lets slip
while stoking the jukebox. Nobody looks
twice at the guy being given the bum's rush;
my legend melts down to a tiny blip,
a half-tone dot on album sleeves, in books.

I retrace my own trail and wipe it dead.
The scene is how I left it. Carefully
I ease myself back down among the wreck's
ice-dusted cache – the dials the crew misread,
the Bopper's dice and Ritchie's crucifix –
and wait for history.

The Sleep Of Estates

In living rooms where fathers sprawl, still clothed,
the bumpy core beyond Sinatra's voice
beats inside a radiogram, a pulse
deep under. There's rain on the windows.

The last buses have left their termini,
each destination cranked to a blank stare.
The grilles that scented underpass and square
have wound down now after the final fry.

The hour belongs to slamming taxi doors,
the clack of heels and laughter in the night;
while mothers wait for clubs to empty out
and faulty street lighting blinks out a morse

that no bare-legged curfew breaker reads.
Young addresses dream of being listed,
double-glazed, damp-coursed, sandblasted,
and rid of roosting seabirds. Overhead

the air is rich with night-time radio,
with baby-listeners, and coded words
that leak from patrol cars and amateurs
across backlanes where cab drivers won't go.

The door shuts soft. The rain has turned to ice.
She lifts the arm out of infinity
in Huyton, and in Skem and Speke and Stockie
née Cantril Farm, so good they named it twice.

Stray

Whatever brought me to the gutter
had something to do with this:
a tree-lined journey to the shop for booze,
paracetamol and papers
where I came across his name
on a photocopied flyer
tacked to the bark of every other trunk.
I soon got to know his sooty coat,
reflective collar. So tenderly written
I half-expected a *Last seen wearing* . . .

Someone had added *Try the Peking Garden*
in shaky freehand. There was a reward
so I started to keep an eye out.
When you asked me what I was thinking
staring through a cloud of midges
those evenings we sat outside drinking
it was usually to do with him –
slowly turning to mulch in deep thicket;
eaten alive by pit bulls;
or his carbon copy, given to a child

who thought him lost to the night.
We'd take in the chairs. I'd sit in the window
listening to far-off sirens
and the sound of my breathing. He was stretching,

getting used to the name they'd given him.
It grew, until one night in September
we ran low on smokes. You sent me to the garage.
I walked down that road with the trees
heavy and still. Hardly a whisper. Turned
past the all-nighter and kept on walking.